A LEGACY OF HONOR

A LEGACY OF HONOR

The Congressional Papers of

Lee H. Hamilton

U.S. House of Representatives 1965–1998
Indiana, Ninth District

Indiana University Libraries
Indiana University Press

This book is a publication of

Indiana University Libraries
Indiana University Press
Herman B Wells Library
1320 East 10th Street
Bloomington, Indiana 47405 USA

Originally published by the Indiana
University Libraries in conjunction with an
exhibition of the papers of Lee H. Hamilton
at the Lilly Library, January 17–April 1,
2006. This updated edition was completed in
January 2019.

Exhibition curated by Kate Cruikshank
Catalog written by Kate Cruikshank

© 2019 by The Trustees of Indiana
University

Manufactured in the United States of
America

ISBN 978-0-253-04611-6

1 2 3 4 5   24 23 22 21 20 19

"Little Hams for Hamilton" campaign parade, 1964

"Whether we're dealing with 9/11 catastrophes, or whether we're dealing with Mideast peace processes, or whether we're dealing with sound electoral systems, he is trusted by the people of our country. Or whether we're providing a forum for bipartisan discussion of the most controversial and important issues, Lee Hamilton is there in the forefront of those efforts and in his quiet way performing in a superb manner. And so the fact that he is a national treasure is something that I hope other Americans share with me as knowledge about Lee Hamilton.

—FORMER PRESIDENT JIMMY CARTER, 1977–1980

With President Jimmy Carter, 1979

CONTENTS

With presidential candidate Robert F. Kennedy at a campaign
rally in Columbus, Indiana, 1966

*"I don't think I came to Washington with the idea that I was going to change the world.
I came to Washington because I thought I could make a positive contribution, not in huge
ways but in small ways, and I think what's driven me was to try to make life better for
Hoosiers, for my constituents. You have to, in the final analysis, hold on to something, and
in my case it's been what helps ordinary people."*

—Lee Hamilton

Driving Lawrenceburg American Legion Post "Pegasus" vehicle
at St. Leon, Indiana, campaign rally, 1968

FOREWORD

This volume commemorates the opening of the Lee H. Hamilton Congressional Papers at Indiana University. The papers are a selection made by his staff from the approximately 3,500 cartons of records generated from 1965 to 1999 during Hamilton's 34-year tenure in the House of Representatives. The collection richly documents Hamilton's emphasis on constituent relations, his continuous concern for the constitutional role of Congress and its proper functioning, and the development of his leadership in U.S. foreign policy.

The collection is also a teaching collection that illustrates how Hamilton's staff prepared legislative background files, how the "whip" system operates, how interest groups approach members of Congress, and how his extensive constituent correspondence was maintained. The teaching nature of this collection is appropriate: From the onset of his congressional tenure, Hamilton's public meetings and newsletters were devoted to clarifying issues rather than advocating positions, helping his constituents to understand problems in all their complexity. His *Washington Report* newsletters and his speeches, both of which are nearly complete in the collection, illustrate the wide range of topics on which he sought to educate both himself and citizens of Indiana's Ninth District.

Although Hamilton did not initially choose involvement in international relations, his early appointment to the Committee on Foreign Affairs and his commitment to becoming informed in all areas for which he had responsibility led quickly to a leadership role as chairman of the Subcommittee on Europe and the Middle East. Approximately 25 cartons of photocopies of his correspondence in that position will eventually provide a resource, normally available only at the National Archives, for exploring the scope of activity undertaken by a member of Congress in the formulation and implementation of foreign policy. (Under House of Representatives rules, such official committee records are restricted until 30 years after creation.)

This book was originally intended to serve as a summary of Hamilton's congressional career, a memento of the 2006 Lilly Library exhibition, and a brief guide to his papers. Since its publication, the IU Libraries have also received from Hamilton his personal 9/11 Commission Papers, the papers of the 9/11 Commission Public Discourse Project, and his Iraq Study Group Papers. The Hamilton collections thus now document not only his distinguished congressional career but his commitment to, and work in support of, the belief that the most pressing national and international problems can be successfully addressed through the nonpartisan work of people of good faith within the context of the American form of representative democracy.

KATE CRUIKSHANK
POLITICAL PAPERS SPECIALIST
INDIANA UNIVERSITY LIBRARIES

With United Nations Ambassador Madeline Albright, 1985

"[He is] one of the few people who understood the challenges of the Cold War era and now truly understands a whole new set of challenges, such as terrorism, global warming, drugs, and a whole host of more countries to deal with than we ever had before."

—MADELEINE ALBRIGHT, SECRETARY OF STATE, 1997–2001

With Vice Premier Deng Xiaoping of the People's Republic of China, 1979

PREFACE

Lee Hamilton has a long and proud relationship with Indiana University, and when he announced his decision in 1998 to donate his papers to the university, we at the Indiana University Libraries were particularly appreciative. By entrusting us with the papers of his extraordinary legislative career he bestowed a great honor.

The IU Libraries and Representative Hamilton have a mutual interest in preserving, studying, displaying, and promoting this collection. With this guide and the accompanying exhibition at the Lilly Library we advance our shared goal.

The papers, as you will discover from this publication, include correspondence, speeches, newsletters, committee minutes, schedules, and legislative research files. A vast resource, they offer endless inspiration for teaching and research, and we are pleased to make them available to scholars and Indiana citizens. Serving Hoosiers in this way is consistent with the long-standing mission of the IU Libraries to provide information to the academic community and beyond.

Libraries are built book by book, collection by collection. The rich collection of Representative Hamilton's congressional papers is an outstanding addition to a library system widely regarded as one of the nation's best. We proudly celebrate the Hamilton papers among our finest treasures.

PATRICIA A. STEELE
RUTH LILLY INTERIM DEAN OF UNIVERSITY LIBRARIES
2006

With Secretary of State Henry Kissinger, 1973

"He's one of those persons who thinks and articulates critical issues in a deliberate fashion, a calm dispassionate presentation of something that he may feel very passionately about at a time when other people might approach the same subject with anger or even with hatred in this day and age."

—Birch Bayh, Senator from Indiana, 1963–1980

With Birch Bayh at St. Leon, Indiana, pole-raising, 1968

THE EXHIBITION

The exhibition "A Legacy of Honor" lays out the major dimensions of Lee Hamilton's congressional career and provides a glimpse into the contents of his congressional papers. Occupying 21 displays in the Lilly Library Main Gallery, the exhibition is divided into three areas of emphasis: Hamilton's relationships with and service to his Ninth-District constituents; his ever-increasing role in foreign policy and foreign affairs; and the workings of Congress and Hamilton's lifelong commitment to making it the institution the founding fathers intended. This last emphasis extends the exhibition into Hamilton's ongoing post-congressional career.

Of particular importance to Hamilton's contact with his constituents were frequent visits to his district and the office procedures he developed to provide nearly immediate responses to constituents. This contact, along with the various ways in which he elicited opinions from constituents and provided information to them, is also captured by the exhibition. A rich array of photos and a comprehensive collection of campaign memorabilia indicate Hamilton's involvement in the life of his district.

Hamilton's involvement in foreign policy is traced from his early chairmanships of two subcommittees of the Committee on Foreign Affairs (Near East, 1971–74, and Investigations, 1975–76). He began to examine in earnest the appropriate congressional role in foreign policy through his long chairmanship of the Subcommittee on Europe and the Middle East (1977– 1994). The exhibition documents the challenges of the Reagan era, when congressional mandates were circumvented, and Hamilton's chairmanship of the House committee investigating the Iran-Contra affair in 1987. His important behind-the-scenes roles in the search for peace in the Middle East and in defining an appropriate role for the United States in the Persian Gulf carry this part of the exhibition up through his retirement. Photographs reveal his cordial relations with a wide array of world leaders.

A portion of the exhibition focuses on how Congress works; it considers the importance of warm bipartisan personal relationships, the role of staff, the critical role of committees and subcommittees, and some of the internal organization behind activity on the floor. The exhibition presents a commitment to the internal reform of Congress that extends beyond Hamilton's congressional career to his position as director of the Center on Congress at Indiana University, established in 1999 and dedicated to educational and outreach activities. The exhibition concludes with his vice chairmanship of the 9/11 Commission and some of the honors and tributes he continues to receive.

Items in the exhibition come from the Lee H. Hamilton Congressional Papers, supplemented by photographs from Lee and Nancy Hamilton's private collection and by campaign memorabilia loaned by Nancy Hamilton, Wayne Vance, and Carolyn Eve.

With South African President Nelson Mandela, 1998

"Lee Hamilton always had a strong point of view, but he understands others, and he listens to others. And he understands how the congressional system must work if two parties, two houses, the president are finally coming to some accord."

—RICHARD LUGAR, SENATOR FROM INDIANA, 1977–2013

With Hillary Rodham Clinton, President Clinton, and Nancy Hamilton at White House Christmas Ball, 1998

Lee Herbert Hamilton served the Ninth District of Indiana in the United States House of Representatives from 1965 to January 1999. He was born in Daytona Beach, Florida, on April 20, 1931. His family relocated to Tennessee and then to Indiana, and he attended the public schools in Evansville, where he graduated from Central High School in 1948, winning the coveted Arthur L. Trester award for the combination of fine character and athletic excellence. He attended DePauw University in Greencastle, Indiana, where he studied history, continued his outstanding basketball career, and graduated with honors in 1952. It was at DePauw that he met his wife, Nancy Ann Nelson; they were married in 1954.

After a year of scholarship study at the Goethe University in Frankfurt am Main, Germany, in 1952–1953, Hamilton entered the Indiana University Law School at IU Bloomington, graduating in 1956. He went into private practice, first in Chicago and then in Columbus, Indiana, where the three Hamilton children, Tracy Lynn, Deborah Lee, and Douglas Nelson, were born. He was chairman of the Bartholomew County Citizens for Kennedy in 1960 and treasurer of the Bartholomew County Young Democrats in 1960–63, then its president from 1963 to 1964. He managed Birch Bayh's Senate campaign in Bartholomew County in 1962 and was persuaded to run for Congress in 1964. After winning that election, he was sent back for 16 additional terms from a district that ostensibly belonged to the Republican Party, in part because of his independent

voting record—socially progressive and fiscally responsible—but above all for his unflagging attention to the needs and concerns of his constituents. He was considered a moderate and independent Democratic congressman.

Indiana's Ninth District

Lee Herbert Hamilton served the Ninth District of Indiana in the U.S. House of Representatives from 1965 to January 1999. The Ninth District in 1964 consisted of 14 counties in southeastern Indiana: Bartholomew, Brown, Dearborn, Franklin, Jackson, Jefferson, Jennings, Lawrence, Ohio, Orange, Ripley, Scott, Switzerland, and Washington. It had 290,596 residents, 31.4 percent below the state district average of 417,523. With a redistricting in 1965, the first in 24 years, the Indiana State legislature designed the map in a way that gave Hamilton more Democratic support, although he would have won reelection in 1966 without the additional votes. Losing Brown County but adding Clark, Decatur, Fayette, and Shelby Counties in 1965, the Ninth District's population was increased to 424,933. Another redistricting in 1968 dropped Orange and Shelby Counties, but added Floyd County, a predominantly Democratic area that raised Hamilton's constituency to 449,200 people. Further redistricting in 1971 added Brown and Harrison Counties, plus seven townships from Monroe County and two from Union County, for a total population of 472,321.

Hamilton family, 1968

With a 1981 redistricting by the Indiana State legislature, Bartholomew County, where Hamilton had his official residence and main district office, was shifted to another district. Hamilton moved both residence and office and was reelected with 67 percent of the vote. The new Ninth District included the whole counties of Brown, Clark, Dearborn, Dubois, Floyd, Franklin, Harrison, Jackson, Jefferson, Jennings, Ohio, Perry, Ripley, Scott, Switzerland, and Union plus townships in the counties of Bartholomew, Crawford, Fayette, Monroe, and Washington, encompassing 6,107 square miles with a total population of 544,936.

The 1990 census brought a further shift. The district now included all of the counties of Brown, Clark, Crawford, Dearborn, Dubois, Floyd, Harrison, Jackson, Jefferson, Jennings, Ohio, Perry, Ripley, Scott, Spencer, Switzerland, Union, and Washington, plus parts of Bartholomew, Fayette, and Franklin, for a total population of 554,416. By 1995 the boundaries had been shifted to include all of Fayette and Franklin.

The Ninth District has no central city population; the only major cities are across the Ohio River in Kentucky and Ohio. The district's population centers have traditionally been New Albany (Floyd County) and Jeffersonville (Clark County), just across the river from Louisville, and most of the industry that existed tended to be along the river as well. Rural problems were acute early in Hamilton's tenure. Farmers were being forced out of business, and the lack of jobs led to migration to cities outside the district. Communities faced imminent decline. The 1970 census counted 150,905 homes, of which 14,034 were without some or all plumbing. In the early 1970s only two of the district's counties met the federal guideline of one physician per 1,000 inhabitants; the Ninth District average was one per 1,500 residents. The uncertain future of large military bases scheduled for closure was also a constant concern during Hamilton's career, bringing both economic and environmental challenges to the district.

Constituent Service

Hamilton's popularity as a Congressman was grounded solidly in his concern for and communication with residents of the Ninth District. His constituents liked him, said one resident whose remark was included in the *Ralph Nader Congress Project* (Grossman Publishers, 1972), "because he talks to them." Talk to them he did, returning to his district at least 40 weekends of every year throughout his career. So dependable was Hamilton's intense district visit schedule that when he took a vacation with his family in August 1971, a press release was issued to account for his absence.

"Lee H. Hamilton Special" truck, 1968

Upon his election to Congress in 1964, Hamilton immediately established a district office in Seymour. By the end of his first year, he had accomplished his goal of visiting every one of the 121 post offices in the sprawling rural district. By March 1967 he had stimulated enough constituent activity to merit moving a staff person from his Washington office to the district office. Just one year later, a second office was opened in Jeffersonville. By June 1970 demand merited two full-time district staff members, and the Seymour office was moved to expanded quarters in the Columbus Post Office; both offices were open for more than 40 hours a week. In October 1973 Hamilton introduced his new "mobile office," a van that would allow him to travel the district with more flexibility than the previous practice of scheduling meetings at post offices. In April 1976 he set up an office in Aurora as well.

By 1977 computer technology made an office reorganization possible. The Washington, D.C., and Columbus offices were linked by computers and all casework was shifted to two full-time caseworkers in Columbus, who from September 1979 handled all work dealing with local, regional, and community projects. The Jeffersonville office was relocated to the post office in May 1980. In the wake of the redistricting in 1981 that put both Hamilton's Columbus office and his personal residence outside his district, the staff and operations of the Columbus office were moved to Jeffersonville. This prompted a move into expanded quarters in spring 1982. The office now handled all project work, casework, and Indiana scheduling. A smaller office was maintained in Aurora until January 1983, when a toll-free number was installed in the Jeffersonville office to make it accessible to all of his constituents.

From early in his career, Hamilton was intent on identifying the needs of his constituents and bringing federal funding to Indiana. In 1966 he undertook with his district staff a study of federal funding to the counties in his district, writing to all federal agencies and exploring the possibilities of federal support for badly needed infra, structure and community and economic development projects. He began holding local conferences and fact-finding meetings with particular interest groups—community development leaders, welfare directors, health workers, educators, students, veterans, farmers, small business owners, women, and senior citizens—that would continue throughout his congressional career. These meetings were not only to ascertain needs but also to gather information on how federal programs were functioning. This was an oversight role upon which he put great emphasis. At the end of his many local meetings and conferences, Hamilton's staff handed out postcards to those people whose questions could not be addressed in the time allotted and encouraged them to send their questions or concerns in writing. Their questions, like all constituent correspondence, were to be answered within 24 hours. In September 1973 Hamilton participated in a monthly telephone hook-up with the Connersville High School senior class, and in January

Hamilton family in parade, 1969

1975 he initiated a several-month series of "Talk with Your Congressman" meetings in counties throughout the district. When Hamilton became vice chair of the Joint Economic Committee in 1983, he held committee field hearings in Indianapolis to consider the rural economy of Indiana.

Annual, biennial, and special interest questionnaires were sent out to elicit constituent opinions on issues before Congress, which helped Hamilton determine his legislative focus. Responses from these surveys grew from 9,000 in 1966 to nearly 15,800 in 1969; they consistently remained above 15,000 over the years. His constituent mail grew similarly, reaching a high of more than 35,000 letters a year by the 1980s and a total of over 50,000 constituent contacts in 1993. Every letter received a focused and meaningful response, taking advantage of computer technology as it emerged.

In addition to responses to specific constituents, Hamilton's side of the conversation also took the form of mailings and newsletters. These general and multi-topic missives quickly developed into his *Washington Report*, which contained substantive, nonpartisan explorations of important issues. Single-spaced and on legal-size paper, often printed on both sides, the *Washington Report* was sent to lists of interested constituents, to all the newspapers in the Ninth District, and to select recipients within the federal government. They were also often read into the *Congressional Record* as a way of stimulating legislative discussion. In addition to treating major domestic and foreign policy issues, topics included how casework is handled, the multiple roles of a Congress member, how best to write to a Congress member, the constitutional roles of the Congress in oversight and foreign policy, the importance of openness and accountability in government, and the need for bureaucratic reform. In 1968 he also began a series of topical radio broadcasts, and the first of what would become a consistent schedule of newspaper and journal articles appeared.

Legislation

Hamilton's constituent relations fed directly into his legislative work. Concerns expressed by constituents often resulted in bills that he initiated in the areas of government operations, economic development, crime, drug abuse, and environmental protection. As he became influential in foreign affairs and national economic policy, he maintained a record of legislation intended to benefit Hoosiers as well as the nation. Hamilton's vision in national and international affairs grew, leading him to support legislation promoting democracy and market reform in the former Soviet Union and Eastern Europe, peace and stability in the Middle East, expanded U.S. markets and trade overseas, and better U.S. export and foreign aid policies. Through his position on the Joint Economic Committee he focused on long-term growth and development, global market competition, and sound fiscal policy. Throughout his career, he supported legislation that would ensure the

Staff meeting, 1978

efficiency and integrity of Congress through ethics, administrative, and organizational reforms. He was consistently against war and adamantly in favor of exhausting all diplomatic options before resorting to force.

Hamilton was a patient and persistent legislator and pursued his causes through multiple sessions of Congress. From the beginning of his congressional career, he gained the respect of his colleagues, building consensus through his advocacy of a wide range of legislative issues. In his first year in Congress, Hamilton was chosen as president of the 89th Congress Democratic freshman class. A year later, he was named Outstanding Freshman Congressman by the Capitol Hill Young Democratic Club for displaying "the characteristics of an effective Congressman: familiarity with the legislation that comes to the House floor; ardent committee work, and responsiveness to his constituents" (press release, January 18, 1966). In March 1971 he was elected by the House Democratic leadership to be one of 18 regional whips that met weekly to discuss upcoming legislation, assess the views of other Democratic House members, and ensure that all members of Congress were present for votes. In this capacity, he was responsible for the other four Indiana Democrats and the representative from Alaska.

Congressional Committee Service

Hamilton's committee service was extensive. In January 1965 he was appointed to the Committee on Foreign Affairs, on which he served until his retirement. In March of that same year, he was appointed to the Subcommittee on the Far East and Pacific, then to the Subcommittee on Europe. In January 1967 he was appointed to the Post Office and Civil Service Committee, which provided the opportunity not only to address the postal needs of his constituents but also to work against burgeoning paperwork and regulations in the federal government. He helped guide through Congress the Postal Reorganization Act of 1970, which created an independent postal service.

In March 1971 he became chairman of the Subcommittee on the Near East, leading him into a lasting and intense engagement with the issues of that region of the world. This leadership role also launched his efforts toward building a more activist role for committees and Congress in the conduct of foreign policy, particularly in using hearings to provide information and in advising the executive branch. In 1973 he became the chair of the new Subcommittee on the Near East and South Asia and in 1975 was elected chair of the Special Subcommittee on Investigations. From the latter position he launched what would become an ongoing examination of the appropriate role of Congress in foreign policy. That same year he was named to the Joint Economic Committee, in part because of his Committee on Foreign Affairs leadership, and began to scrutinize the relationship between the U.S. economy and U.S. foreign policy.

Committee on Foreign Affairs, 1986

With the opening of the 95th Congress in 1977, Hamilton became chair of the Committee on Foreign Affairs Subcommittee on Europe and the Middle East, a position he held until 1995. In addition, he took on the issue of congressional ethics with appointments to both the Committee on Standards of Official Conduct and to the House Select Committee on Ethics. He was also named to the Commission on Administrative Review, which began hearings in January 1977 on congressional staff, structure, and labor practices.

In 1981 Hamilton was named to the House Permanent Select Committee on Intelligence, of which he remained a member for six years, serving as chair in 1985–86. He was vice chair of the Joint Economic Committee for both the 98th and 99th Congresses (1983–86).

With the opening of the 100th Congress in 1987, Hamilton was named to chair the House Committee to Investigate Covert Arms Transactions with Iran (Iran-Contra), which would dominate his time and the attention of the country for the better part of the year. He also became a member of the Committee on Science, Space, and Technology. With the opening of the 101st Congress in 1989, he became chair of the Joint Economic Committee.

Hamilton introduced legislation in July 1991 to create the Joint Committee on the Organization of Congress to undertake a comprehensive examination of internal operations, for which he argued strenuously—and ultimately, successfully—over the ensuing year. In August, the Speaker of the House named him to chair the October Surprise Task Force of the Committee on Foreign Affairs, created in response to public pressure to investigate whether Reagan campaign officials had deliberately intervened in the Iran hostage negotiations in order to ensure the defeat of Jimmy Carter in 1980. The investigation lasted through 1992, overlapping with Hamilton's appointment in August 1992 as co–chair of the Joint Committee on the Organization of Congress. Hamilton chaired the full Committee on Foreign Affairs for the 103rd Congress (1993–94). During the 104th and 105th Congresses he remained a member of the Joint Economic Committee and was the ranking minority member of the Committee on Foreign Affairs upon his retirement in January 1999.

With Lech Walesa, head of the Polish Solidarity movement, 1989

Other Congressional Service

Hamilton served Congress in other capacities as well. He was named in June 1968 to a bipartisan congressional steering committee, arranged by the U.S. Conference of Mayors and funded by the Ford Foundation, to oversee studies of the problems of urban areas. In 1971 he began extended participation in the Congressional Delegation of the U.S. Group of the Inter-Parliamentary Union and in 1983 became a member of its Executive Committee. In support of his Committee on Foreign Affairs work he traveled extensively, including trips to Southeast Asia in June 1970, to the Middle East in November 1982, and to Panama in January 1990.

Post-Congressional Career

Upon leaving Congress in 1999, Hamilton became director of the Woodrow Wilson International Center for Scholars in Washington, D.C., where scholars, policy makers, and business leaders engage in a comprehensive and nonpartisan dialogue on public policy issues, their historical backgrounds, and their effect on national and international thought and governance. He was subsequently also named president and served in that dual capacity until 2010.

Working the IU President Myles Brand, Hamilton established the Center on Congress at Indiana University, which opened in January 1999. The Center was directed by Hamilton until 2015 and was a nonpartisan educational institution designed to explain the work and role of Congress to the general public and to improve civic engagement, especially among young people, as a way to strengthen basic American institutions of government. In 2015 the Center was incorporated into the IU Center on Representative Government, for which Hamilton continues to publish a bi-weekly "Comments on Congress" electronic newsletter available via e-mail to interested citizens and disseminated regularly to district and regional newspapers.

Hamilton has remained an important and active voice on matters of international relations and foreign affairs, serving as a commissioner on the influential United States Commission on National Security in the 21st Century (better known as the Hart Rudman Commission), and as co-chair with former Senator Howard Baker on the Baker-Hamilton Commission to Investigate Certain Security Issues at Los Alamos. He also served as a member of the advisory council for the U.S. Department of Homeland Security beginning in 2001, and from December 2002 through August 2004 he served as vice chairman of the National Commission on Terrorist Attacks upon the United States, known as the 9/11 Commission, which has been widely recognized as a model of excellence for commission work in terms of process and bipartisanship. He spearheaded creation of the 9/11 Public Discourse Project growing out of the commission's work, advocating relentlessly with his fellow commissioners in support of the National Intelligence Reform

In Panama with General Thurmond of the U.S. Southern Command, 1990

Honorary doctorate speech, American University, 1991

With Nancy Hamilton and Presidents Ford, Carter, and George H.W. Bush, 1998

Act, which was signed into law in December 2004, and for reform of congressional oversight of intelligence matters. He was appointed to the President's Foreign Intelligence Advisory Board in November 2005.

With former Senator Spencer Abraham, Hamilton co-chaired the Independent Task Force on Immigration and America's Future, which issued a report in 2006 laying out a plan for comprehensive immigration reform. During the Barack Obama presidency he served on the President's Foreign Intelligence Advisory board and the President's Homeland Security Advisory Council. He is an honorary chair of the World Justice Project and currently serving as co-chair of the United States Institute of Peace Task Force to Prevent Extremism in Fragile States

In 2013 Hamilton was appointed a Professor of Practice in the School of Public and Environmental Affairs and a Distinguished Scholar in the School of Global and International Studies at Indiana University. In October 2018 the latter was renamed the Lee H. Hamilton and Richard G. Lugar School of Global and International Studies to honor Hamilton and his Senate colleague, Richard G. Lugar, for their outstanding work in international relations. He received the Presidential Medal of Freedom from President Barack Obama in 2015 and was awarded the University Medal by Indiana University President Michael McRobbie in 2018.

Hamilton's unrelenting advocacy for a stronger congressional role in foreign policy and for greater public awareness of and concern for the work of Congress have been expressed in four books published after his retirement from Congress:

- A *Creative* Tension: *The Foreign Policy Roles of the President and Congress*. Washington D.C.: Woodrow Wilson Press, distributed by Johns Hopkins Press, 2002.
- *How Congress Works and Why You Should Care*. Bloomington, Indiana: Indiana University Press, 2004.
- *Strengthening Congress*. Bloomington, Indiana: Indiana University Press, 2009.
- *Congress, Presidents, and American Politics: Fifty Years of Writings and Reflections*. Bloomington, Indiana: Indiana University Press, 2016.

His commitment to the potential of bipartisan collaboration to solve the nation's most intractable problems is articulated in *Without Precedent: The Inside Story of the 9/11 Commission*, co-authored with co-chair Thomas H. Kean and special assistant Benjamin Rhodes (New York: Alfred A. Knopf, 2006).

With Saudi Arabian Oil Minister Sheik Yamani, 1977

"Lee Hamilton's the one man who is called upon repeatedly by contemporary people in government to take on the tough issues, the big issues, the ones that call for an uncommon amount of ethics and integrity, where no hint of partisanship is going to smear whatever findings his committee or commission or his speech comes out with. In that regard he's an extraordinarily uncommon public servant."

—JERRY UDELL, FORMER HAMILTON STAFF MEMBER

St. Leon, Indiana, pole-raising, 1968

Lee H. Hamilton
Congressional Papers
1965–1999
270 linear feet (219 cartons)

Overview of the Collection

The Lee H. Hamilton Congressional papers are a selection from the approximately 3500 cartons of records generated during his 34-year tenure in the House of Representatives. The contents of the collection, chosen by his staff, illustrate the multiple roles of a model Congressman, i.e. local representative and constituent advocate, represented in the Legislative and Constituent Services series; national legislator and consensus builder, reflected in the Legislative series; educator, evident in the Public Communications series; committee member, reflected in his impressive record of committee service but particularly in the Committee on Foreign Affairs series; and investigator, again evident in his committee service but with special emphasis in the series on the Iran-Contra investigation of 1987.

A major strength of the collection lies in its portrayal of Hamilton's consistently strong record of service to his constituents both in projects of many kinds throughout the 9th district and his emphasis on personalized responses to constituent correspondence that by 1989 was numbering close to 30,000 letters a year. He developed his positions on legislative issues in part through his substantive responses to those correspondents,

which are to be found in the Legislative Mail and Issues Files subseries. The mechanisms through which that level of communication was maintained are evident in the Alphas and Form Letters subseries, the Schedule Files, and the Weekly Reports, all in the Office Administration series. The Schedule Files in the Office Administration series are a rich resource for his face-to-face contacts with constituents. The content of Hamilton's side of the dialogue is richly represented in his weekly *Washington Reports* newsletters, Mailings, and Speeches in the Public Communications series as well as in the Extensions of Remarks and Statements subseries of the Legislative series. The *Washington Reports* as well as his *Foreign Affairs Newsletters* are available in digital form through the finding aid for the collection.

Resources for studying constituent positions are likewise quite plentiful, particularly for the early 1970s, for which there are nearly 34 linear feet of letters on specific legislation as well as local, national, and international issues of concern. Letters on the possible impeachment of Nixon, the energy crisis, and such continuing issues as abortion and drugs are particularly abundant.

The Projects subseries of the Constituent Services series offers particular potential for research because of both its extent and because of the abundance of records in certain portions of the subseries. The threat of base closures hovered over nearly the full span of Hamilton's career, with the consequent economic displacement and environmental problems. The records for the Jefferson Proving Ground in particular (7.5 linear feet), as well as for the Bakalar Air Force Base, the Indiana Army Ammunition Plant, and the Naval Ordnance Station in Louisville, trace not only Hamilton's efforts but the mobilization of local initiatives to exert pressure on numerous parts of the federal bureaucracy in order to humanize the process and the ultimate disposition of those installations. Broader coverage is available in other portions of the Projects files, supplemented by the files on Indiana Projects and Issues from the 1980s, found in the Research-News Clippings 1979–1986 subseries of the Constituent Services series. The Projects subseries also offers abundant resources for researching the specific environmental issues associated with flood control, watersheds, Ohio River development and pollution, nuclear power, and the pollution of unexploded ordnance at the Jefferson Proving Ground. There are also abundant resources on the evolution of proposals for the Hoosier National Forest and the Muscatatuck Wildlife Refuge in the Wilderness records of the Projects subseries.

Another strength of the collection lies in its reflection of Hamilton's emphasis on the integrity of the institution of Congress and its constitutional role, to be found in his work with the Commission on Administrative Review, the Committee on Standards of Official Conduct, and the Joint Committee on the Organization of Congress, and throughout his career in his work with the Committee on Foreign Affairs, as he built the foundations for a more active congressional role in the formulation of foreign policy. The records relating to the Committee on Foreign Affairs are an additional strength of the collection and will become more so over time as they are opened. The photocopies of official correspondence and memoranda are governed by House of Representatives Rule VII, which restricts access to them until 30 years from date of creation. Also of interest are the files relating to the hearings of the House Select Committee to Investigate Covert Arms Transactions with Iran (Iran-Contra), for which there is a daily record of journalistic coverage from the *New York Times*, the *Washington Post*, and the *Christian Science Monitor* as well as hearings materials in both preliminary and printed form.

An online guide to the collection is available through Archives Online at Indiana University:

(http://webapp1.dlib.indiana.edu/findingaids /view?docId=VAA2020.xml&brand= general&startDoc=21).

Election night, 1964

"His word is his bond. I'd trust him with my life, with my family, and, of course, with my country."

—BIRCH BAYH, SENATOR FROM INDIANA, 1963–1980

Democrat-Republican baseball game, with Birch Bayh, 1967

Lee H. Hamilton
9/11 Commission Papers
2003–2005
10 linear feet (8 cartons)

Historical Note

The National Commission on Terrorist Attacks Upon the United States, also known as the 9/11 Commission, was an independent, bipartisan commission created by congressional legislation and the signature of President George W. Bush in late 2002. It was chartered to prepare a full and complete account of the circumstances surrounding the September 11, 2001, terrorist attacks on the World Trade Center and the Pentagon, including preparedness for and the immediate response to the attacks. The Commission was also mandated to provide recommendations designed to guard against future attacks.

Chair of the Commission was former New Jersey Governor (1982–1990) Thomas Kean, Vice Chair was former Indiana 9th district Congressman (1965–1998) Lee H. Hamilton. The other commissioners were Richard Ben-Veniste, Fred F. Fielding, Jamie S. Gorelick, Slade Gorton, Bob Kerrey, John F. Lehman, Timothy J. Roemer, and James R. Thompson. A staff of 81 was led by Philip D. Zelikow as Executive Director, Christopher A. Kojm as Deputy Executive Director, and Daniel Marcus as Chief Counsel. Although consisting of five Democrats and five Republicans, Kean and Hamilton

agreed from the outset that the process would be nonpartisan and that recommendations would be arrived at by consensus. Hamilton's commitment to this process appears to have been the impetus to compiling his personal historical record contained in the collection.

Because of the scope of the work, staff was divided into 9 teams (later slightly reorganized) to investigate Al Qa'ida and Related Transnational Terrorist Groups; Intelligence Collection, Analysis, Management, Oversight, and Resources; International Counter-Terrorism Policy; Terrorist Financing; Border Security and Foreign Visitors; Law Enforcement and Intelligence Efforts Inside the U.S.; Commercial Aviation and Transportation Security; National Leadership: Immediate Response, Crisis Management, and Continuity of Government; and Emergency Response and Consequence Management: New York City and the Pentagon.

The Commission held an inaugural public hearing March 31–April 1, 2003, providing through testimony an overview of the range of the investigation, then 11 more public hearings in the next 14 months focusing on Congress and Civil Aviation Security; Terrorism, al Qaeda, and the Muslim World; Intelligence and the War on Terrorism; Private/Public Sector Partnerships for Emergency Preparedness; Security and Liberty; Borders, Transportation, and Managing Risk; Counterterrorism Policy;

testimony from Condoleezza Rice; Law Enforcement and Intelligence; Emergency Response; and The 9/11 Plot and National Crisis Management.

On July 22, 2004, the Commission released its public report, published in a paperback run of 500,000 by W. W. Norton and priced at $10 in the hope that every American would be able to afford it.

The Commission's mandate expired August 21, 2004. On that date, staff monographs on Terrorist Financing and on 9/11 and Terrorist Travel were released, accompanied eventually by 17 staff reports on various aspects of the Commission's investigations. The National Archives maintains a website on the 9/11 Commission that provides links to these publications for download, as well as biographical information on the commissioners.

Overview of the Collection

The record that Hamilton assembled in this collection documents the inner workings of the 9/11 Commission on a nearly daily basis, including efforts to gain access to White House documents, interactions with the 9/11 families, and ongoing attention to press coverage and speculation. It reveals the intensity of efforts to maintain the integrity of the nonpartisan, reasoned approach to their charge to which Kean and Hamilton had committed themselves and the pressures they confronted in protecting that process.

The Working Documents series comprises approximately half of the collection and consists largely of emails and their attachments, sent among Commissioners and to or from staff. The commission's front office, consisting of the executive director and his deputy, the general counsel and his deputy, the communications director, the special assistant, and the family liaison, ran the daily operations and served as a conduit between the commissioners and staff.

The Hamilton collection is complementary to the official records of the 9/11 Commission, which consist of approximately 570 feet of textual files and an unspecified amount of electronic and audio-visual material and are housed at the National Archives in Washington, D.C.

Most of the collection was received in 2006 in 67 three-ring binders, 37 of them labeled numerically and arranged chronologically and the rest labeled topically. Following as much as possible the categories of arrangement as received, the collection consists of the following series: Briefing Books, Staff Reports, Working Drafts for 9/11 Recommendations, Working Notes (Hamilton's), Team 5: Borders, Staff Statements, Selected Readings, Hamilton's Background Readings, Testimony Binders, and Working Documents. While the basic order within each series is chronological, Hamilton at times grouped documents by theme in preparation for hearings, the writing of the 9/11 Commission Report, or the writing of Without Precedent, the volume on the workings of the 9/11 Commission co-authored by Hamilton and Thomas Kean. The order of these grouped documents has been retained in both the original and digitized collection. Three additional small series received in December 2010, Office Files, Clippings, and Memorabilia, are also arranged chronologically. They have not been digitized.

An online guide to the collection is available through Archives Online at Indiana University:

(http://webapp1.dlib.indiana.edu /findingaids/view?docId=VAB8595 .xml&brand=general&startDoc=21).

With Vice President Walter Mondale, 1977

"In my own view, there is no member in this century who has made a greater contribution to the stability and integrity of our foreign policy than has Lee Hamilton."

—TOM FOLEY, SPEAKER OF THE HOUSE OF REPRESENTATIVES, 1989–1994

With Governor Matt Welsh, Birch Bayh, Ed Roush, and John Brademas at Democratic National Convention, Miami, 1971

**Lee H. Hamilton
9/11 Commission Public Discourse
Project Papers
2003–2007
7.5 linear feet (9 cartons)**

Historical Note

In an effort to maintain pressure on Congress and the Executive branch for implementation of the 9/11 Commission's recommendations and to build public support, the ten commissioners created the 9/11 Public Discourse Project, which continued through December 31, 2005.

The PDP was established as a non-profit tax-exempt organization, with the ten members of the 9/11 Commission serving as its board of directors. Originally conceived as a one-year project, it was supported in its first year largely by the William and Flora Hewlett Foundation. Under the directorship of Christopher Kojm, who had served as deputy to 9/11 Commission vice-chair Lee Hamilton, the commissioners undertook extensive congressional testimony and public appearances.

As it became clear that the work of implementation was going to be a great deal more complex than anticipated, they sought funding for additional time, provided by the Knight Foundation and by a grant from the Smith Richardson Foundation. Their seven public sessions on "The Unfinished Agenda" in June and July 2005 were a prelude to the intensive reports on implementation in fall 2005, culminating in December with the widely publicized "report card" sessions that graded the executive and legislative branches of government as well as relevant law enforcement agencies on their implementation of the recommendations in the 9/11 Commission's report. The project ceased operation on December 31, 2005. Lee Hamilton and his staff continued to document their work during the course of the project, which documentation is captured in this collection.

Overview of the Collection

The collection consists of Director Christopher Kojm's office files; briefing books, notes, and presentation materials for The Unfinished Agenda and other public report sessions on the status of the 9/11 Commission recommendations; testimony by Lee Hamilton and others before Congress regarding implementation of the recommendations; the typescript for Lee Hamilton and Thomas Kean's book Without Precedent; Lee Hamilton's emails and working notes for the duration of the 9/11 Public Discourse Project and beyond, from September 1, 2004, through June 2006; working documents consisting of emails and their attachments; and tapes and props from the public report sessions.

This collection is a continuation of the Lee H. Hamilton 9/11 Commission Papers, with the working documents picking up on August 22, 2004, the day after the Commission's mandate expired. While the 9/11 Public Discourse Project went out of existence in December 2005, this collection contains documents up through 2010 as they apply to the 9/11 Commission.

An online guide to the collection is available through Archives Online at Indiana University:

(http://webapp1.dlib.indiana.edu/findingaids/view?docId=VAC1262.xml&brand=general&startDoc=21).

A campaign rally for Lee Hamilton in Columbus, Indiana, with Robert F. Kennedy and Birch Bayh, 1966

"If were to advise the Almighty as to how He puts together a perfect member of Congress, to represent the people on one hand and to deal with the humongous problems that confront our country and confront the world, I think I'd ask the good Lord to take a look at Lee Hamilton and see if He can't make a whole bunch of people just like he is."

—BIRCH BAYH, SENATOR FROM INDIANA, 1963–1980

Groundbreaking for the Markland Dam with Kentucky Congressman Gene Snyder and Indiana Governor Otis Bowen, 1975

Honors and Awards

Hamilton has received numerous honors and awards for his congressional and post-congressional service. He has received honorary degrees from the following colleges and universities:

American University
Anderson University
Ball State University
Bellarmine University
DePauw University
Detroit College of Law
Franklin College
Georgetown University School of Law
Hanover College
Indiana State University
Indiana University
Marian College
Shenandoah University
Suffolk University
Union College
University of Indianapolis
University of Southern Indiana
Wabash College

Among his state, regional, national, and international awards and honors are the following:

Indiana University's University Medal, 2018

Naming of the Lee H. Hamilton and Richard G. Lugar School of Global and International Studies, 2018

Presidential Medal of Freedom, 2015

The Episcopal Diocese and the Commission on Peace 2005 Peacemaker Award, November 2005

Virginia Military Institute Distinguished Diplomat Award, November 2005

U.S. Capitol Historical Society, 2005 Freedom Award, November 2005

Smith College Arnold D. and Judith S. Friedman '26 Fellowship Fund Lecturer, October 2005

Wesleyan University Raymond E. Baldwin Lecturer, October 2005

The Franklin and Eleanor Roosevelt Institute Freedom From Fear Award, with Governor Thomas Kean, October 2005

The National Conference on Citizenship 2005 Citizen of the Year Award, September 2005

The Frank O'Bannon Public Service Award, August 2005

Indiana Historical Society Living Legends Award, July 2005

The Junior Statesmen Foundation Statesman of the Year with Governor Thomas Kean, July 2005

The Jefferson Award for Public Service, June 2005

Distinguished Citizen Fellow, Institute for Advanced Study, Indiana University, April 2005

TIME magazine "People Who Mattered 2004" with Governor Thomas Kean, December 27, 2004

Americans for More Civility 2004 Civic Award with Governor Thomas Kean, December 2004

Distinguished Public Service Award, Center for Congressional and Presidential Studies, American University, November 2004

2004 Building Bridges Award, Voices of September 11, October 2004

Rotary Foundation of Rotary International Paul Harris Fellow, April 2004

Eisenhower National Security Series Award, October 2003

The UCLA Medal, May 2003

Butler University President's Medal, April 2003

Washingtonian magazine's "Washington's Wise Men," November 2001

Richard W. Leopold Lectureship, Northwestern University, October 2001

American Foreign Service Association Lifetime Contribution to American Diplomacy, June 2001

Conner Prairie "Spirit of the Prairie" Award, April 2001

Presidential envoy to Taiwan, March 2000

Daughters of the American Revolution Medal of Honor, 1999

American Task Force for Lebanon Philip Habib Award for Distinguished Public Service, 1999

Knight Commander's Cross of the Order of Merit of the Federal Republic of Germany, 1999

Indiana Humanities Council Lifetime Achievement Award, 1999

Human Endeavor Award for Service to Rural Indiana, Hoosier Energy, Inc., 1999

Paul H. Nitze Award for Distinguished Authority on National Security Affairs, 1999

National Rural Electric Cooperative Association Distinguished Service Award, 1999

Indiana University Southeast Chancellor's Medallion, 1999

U.S. Association of Former Members of Congress Statesmanship Award, 1999

Delphi International 1999 International Cooperation Award

Department of Defense Medal for Distinguished Public Service, 1998

Election to the American Academy of Diplomacy, 1998

International Research and Exchange Board Distinguished Career Award, 1998

American Political Science Association Hubert H. Humphrey Award, 1998

Jefferson/Clark Counties NAACP Heritage Award, 1998

American Bar Association Central and Eastern European Law Initiative Award, 1998

Bread for the World Seeds of Hope Award, 1998

Center for Civic Education Civitas Award, 1998

DePauw University Old Gold Medal, 1998

Columbus Human Rights Commission William R. Laws Human Rights Award, 1998

Indiana Chamber of Commerce Government Leader of the Year Award, 1997

Center for National Policy Edmund S. Muskie Distinguished Public Service Award, 1997

American Political Science Association Outstanding Legislator Award, 1997

American Shooting Sports Council Firearms Freedom Award, 1997

Indiana University President's Medal for Excellence, 1996

Republic of Greece Insignia of the Decoration of the Commander of the Order of Phoenix, 1995

Asia-Pacific Council of American Chambers of Commerce Award, 1995

American Business Council of the Gulf Countries Patriot of the Expatriates Award, 1995

Baha'i Humanitarian Award, 1995 Alfalfa Club Member, 1995

Indiana University Institute for Advanced Study Distinguished Citizen Fellow, 1994

Georgetown University Chair for Distinguished Service, 1991

Indiana University School of Law Academy of Alumni Fellows, 1990

Center for the Study of the Presidency Public Service Medal, 1990

American Farm Bureau Federation Golden Plow Award, 1989

Federation of German-American Clubs'
General Lucius D. Clay Award, 1989

Indiana Academy Member, 1989

Midwest Universities Consortium for
International Activities 25th Anniversary
Award, 1989

Central Intelligence Agency Medallion,
1988

Defense Intelligence Agency Medallion,
1987

DePauw University McNaughton Medal for
Public Service, 1987

Indiana Trial Lawyers Association Freedom
Award, 1987

Indiana Bar Association Distinguished
Speaker, 1987

Grand Cross of the Order of Merit of the
Federal Republic of Germany, 1985

Knight of the French Legion of Honor, 1984
Indiana Basketball Hall of Fame, 1982

With Highway Commissioner Curtis A. Wiley and Deputy
Commissioner Dennis Faulkenberg holding Lee H. Hamilton
Highway sign, 1997

"I just see every day the impact of foreign policy and foreign affairs on the lives of ordinary Hoosiers, whether or not they have markets to sell their products, their corn and their soybeans, or whether or not their young men and young women have to go into dangerous places around the world."

—LEE HAMILTON

At a constituent meeting in the Austin, Indiana firehouse, early
1970s

Memberships, Boards, Committees, and Councils

Aequitas International Consulting, Consultant

Albert Shanker Institute, Signatory

Albright-Stonebridge Group Board of Advisors, Member

The American Assembly, Steering Committee

American Council for the United Nations University, Board Member

American-German Council on Public Policy, Board Member

American Police Hall of Fame Distinguished Citizens Advisory Board

American Political Science Association

Advisory Committee for the Congressional Fellowship Program, Member; First Honorary Congressional Fellow

AMIDEAST Honorary Committee for 50th Anniversary Commemoration, Member

Annenberg Public Policy Center, University of Pennsylvania, "Institutions of Democracy," National Advisory Board

Association of the United States Army: Role of American Military Power Project, Advisory Board

BAE Systems, Board of Directors

Bretton Woods Committee, Member

Brookings Institution, Honorary Trustee; Member of the Executive Committee of the Board of Trustees

Center for Strategic and International Studies (CSIS), Distinguished Congressional Fellow

Center for the Study of the Presidency, National Board of Advisors

Claritage Opportunity Fund, LP, Advisory Board

Close Up Foundation, Board of Advisors

Council for Excellence in Government, Board Member

Drug Strategies, Past Board Member; Advisory Board Member

The Education for Employment Foundation, Board Member

Eisenhower Exchange Fellowships, President's Advisory Council

Federal Bureau of Investigation Director's Advisory Board, Member

Ford Foundation's National Selection Committee, Innovations in American Government, Member

Foreign Affairs Museum Council, Board Member

Fulbright Association Selection Committee, Fulbright Prize for International Understanding, Chair

The Fund for Peace, Advisory Council

The German Marshall Fund of the United States, Past Board Member

The German Marshall Fund of the United States National Advisory Committee of American Marshall Memorial Fellowship Program, Member

Global Green USA, Board Member

Goals for Americans Foundation, Board Member

Independent Task Force on Immigration and America's Future, Co-Chair

Institut Choiseul, Member, Academic Board

Institute for the Study of Diplomacy, Board Member

InterAction: American Council for Voluntary International Action, Board Member

Inter-American Dialogue, Member

International Center for Religion and Diplomacy, Member, Board of Advisors

The Internews Channel, Member, Board of Advisors

The John Brademas Center for the Study of Congress, Robert F. Wagner Graduate School of Public Service, New York University, Advisory Council

The National Academies, Committee on Science and Technology to Support Health Care, Sustainability, and Other Aspects of Development Assistance, Member

National Cathedral Association, Advisory Council

National Committee on U.S.-China Relations, Vice Chair, Board of Directors

National Council on U.S.-Indonesia Relations, Co-Chair, Advisory Committee

National Endowment for Democracy, Board Member

Pacific Council on International Policy at University of Southern California, Charter Member

Partnership to Cut Hunger and Poverty in Africa, Michigan State University, Executive Committee Co-Chair

Partnership for a Secure America, Advisory Board Co-Chair

Population Action International, Board Member

The President's Foreign Intelligence Advisory Board, Member

President's Homeland Security Advisory Council, Member

Randall L. Tobias Center for Leadership Excellence, Indiana University, Board Member

U.S.-Asia Pacific Council, Founding Member; Member, Executive Committee

United Nations Association of the United States of America, Board Member

United States Association of Former Members of Congress, Board Member

United States Capitol Historical Society, Board Member

U.S. Department of Homeland Security, Advisory Council Member

University of Pennsylvania Institute for Strategic Threat Analysis and Responses, External Board

Watson Institute for International Studies, Brown University, Board of Overseers

The Washington Center for Internships and Academic Seminars Institute for Civic Leadership, Honorary Co-Chair, Congressional Advisory Committee

The Woodrow Wilson Presidential Library, National Advisory Council

World Affairs Council of Washington, D.C., Advisory Board

World Justice Project, Honorary Chair

In white convertible in North Vernon, Indiana, parade, 1978

"He loves what he does. He always has. He's said time and time again, 'I can't think of anything I would rather have done or would rather do at this time in history.'"

—NANCY HAMILTON

Lee and Nancy Hamilton with President and Mrs. Clinton and the Empress of Japan, 1994

APPENDIX C

Commissions and Panels

Baker-Hamilton Commission to Investigate Certain Security Issues at Los Alamos, Co-Chair

Blue Ribbon Commission on America's Nuclear Future, Co-Chair

Blue Ribbon Commission on Russia and America's National Interest, Member

Carter-Baker Commission on Federal Election Reform, Member

Center for Strategic and International Studies (CSIS) Twenty-First Century Commission on U.S. Foreign Economic Policy in a Globalized Economy, Co-Chair

Columbia University Task Force on Foreign Aid in the 21st Century, Member

Commission on Science and Security, Department of Energy Task Force, Ex-officio Member

Council on Foreign Relations-Freedom House Task Force on U.S. Role in the United Nations, Member

Council on Foreign Relations Independent Task Force on U.S.-Cuban Relations in the 21st Century, Member

Council on Foreign Relations Task Force on the State Department, Member

Department of Energy Russia Task Force, Member

Director of Central Intelligence's Economic Intelligence Advisory Panel, Member

Future International Financial Architecture Task Force, Member

International Commission on Intervention and State Sovereignty, Commissioner

National Commission on Terrorist Attacks upon the United States, Vice Chair

Panetta Institute Scholarship Awards Panel, Member

Secretary of Defense's National Security Study Group, Member

Task Force on Strengthening Palestinian Public Institutions, Member

Task Force on the Future of International Financial Architecture, Member

United States Commission on National Security/21st Century, Commissioner

United States Department of Homeland Security Task Force on Preventing the Entry of Weapons of Mass Effect on American Soil, Member

Yale University Press, Advisory Board for the Culture and Civilization of China Program, Member

With Egyptian President Hosni Mubarak, 1983

"I think one of the things that gave me the greatest satisfaction in the Congress was seeing communities enhanced, the quality of life in those communities, because of things that I had done—to help bring a library to a community, help bring a water system to a community, build a road or a highway or a bridge, or do a thousand and one things that every member of the Congress does. I got a lot of satisfaction out of that."

—LEE HAMILTON

With Queen Elizabeth II at the U.S. Capitol, 1976

APPENDIX D

Committee Service

U.S. House of Representatives, 1965–1998

89th Congress, 1965–66
Foreign Affairs
Subcommittees on:
Far East and Pacific
Europe

90th Congress, 1967–68
Foreign Affairs
Subcommittees on:
Asian and Pacific Affairs
Europe
Inter-American Affairs
Post Office & Civil Service
Subcommittees on:
Manpower and Civil Service
Compensation

91st Congress, 1969–70
Foreign Affairs
Subcommittees on:
Asian and Pacific Affairs
Europe
Inter-American Affairs
Post Office & Civil Service
Subcommittees on:
Manpower and Civil Service
Compensation
Postal Rates

Select Committee on U.S. Involvement in Southeast Asia (June 15–July 5, 1970)

92nd Congress, 1971–72
Foreign Affairs
Subcommittees on:
Asian and Pacific Affairs
Europe
Near East (Chair)
Post Office & Civil Service
Subcommittees on:
Employee Benefits (Chair)
Investigations
Postal Service

93rd Congress, 1973–74
Foreign Affairs
Subcommittees on:
Asian and Pacific Affairs
Europe
Near East and South Asia (Chair)

94th Congress, 1975–76
International Relations
Subcommittees on:
International Economic Policy
Investigations (Chair)
Joint Economic Committee
Subcommittees on:
Economic Progress
Fiscal Policy
Inter-American Economic Relationships
International Economics
Energy (1976 only)

95th Congress, 1977–78
International Relations
Subcommittees on:
Europe and the Middle East (Chair)
International Organizations
Standards of Official Conduct
Select Committee on Ethics (from March 10, 1977)
Commission on Administrative Review
Joint Economic Committee
Subcommittees on:
International Economics
Economic Growth and Stabilization

96th Congress, 1979–80
Foreign Affairs
Subcommittees on:
Europe and the Middle East (Chair)
International Security and Scientific Affairs
Standards of Official Conduct<
Joint Economic Committee
Subcommittees on:
International Economics
Economic Growth and Stabilization
Energy

97th Congress, 1981–82
Foreign Affairs
Subcommittees on:
Europe and the Middle East (Chair)
International Security and Scientific Affairs
Permanent Select Committee on Intelligence (from Feb. 18, 1981)
Joint Economic Committee
Subcommittees on:
Economic Goals and Intergovernmental Policy (Chair)
Monetary and Fiscal Policy

98th Congress, 1983–84
Foreign Affairs
Subcommittees on:
Europe and the Middle East (Chair)
International Security and Scientific Affairs
Permanent Select Committee on Intelligence (from Feb. 18, 1981)
Subcommittees on:
Oversight and Evaluation (1983)
Program and Budget Authorization (1984)
Joint Economic Committee (Vice-Chair)
Subcommittees on:
Economic Goals and Intergovernmental Policy (Chair)
Monetary and Fiscal Policy

99th Congress, 1985–86
Foreign Affairs
Subcommittees on:
Europe and the Middle East (Chair)
Arms, Control, International Security and Science
Permanent Select Committee on Intelligence (Chair)
Subcommittees on:
Legislation
Oversight and Evaluation
Program and Budget Authorization (1985)
Joint Economic Committee (Vice-Chair)
Subcommittees on:
Economic Goals and Intergovernmental Policy (Chair)
Monetary and Fiscal Policy

100th Congress, 1987–88
Foreign Affairs
  Subcommittees on:
    Europe and the Middle East (Chair)
    Arms, Control, International Security
    and Science
**Select Committee to Investigate Covert
Arms Transactions with Iran (Chair)
(Jan. 7–Nov. 17, 1987)**
Science, Space, and Technology
  Subcommittees on:
    Science, Research, and Technology
    International Scientific Cooperation
Joint Economic Committee (Vice-Chair)
  Subcommittees on:
    Economic Goals and Intergovernmen-
    tal Policy (Chair)
    International Economic Policy
    Economic Growth, Trade, and Taxes

101st Congress, 1989–90
Foreign Affairs
  Subcommittee on:
    Europe and the Middle East (Chair)
Science, Space, and Technology
  Subcommittees on:
  Science, Research, and Technology
  International Scientific Cooperation
Joint Economic Committee (Chair)
  Subcommittees on: <
    Economic Goals and Intergovernmen-
    tal Policy (Chair)
    International Economic Policy
    Economic Growth, Trade, and Taxes

102nd Congress, 1991–92
Foreign Affairs
  Subcommittee on:

    Europe and the Middle East (Chair)
**Task Force to Investigate Certain
Allegations Concerning Holding of
Americans as Hostages in Iran in
1980 ["October Surprise" Task Force]
(Chair from August 1991)**
**Joint Economic Committee
(Vice-Chair)**
  Subcommittees on:
    Economic Goals and Intergovernmental
    Policy (Chair)
    International Economic Policy
    Economic Growth, Trade, and
    Taxes
**Joint Committee on the Organization
of Congress (Co-Chair from August
1992)**

103rd Congress, 1993–94
Foreign Affairs (Chair)
  Subcommittee on:
    Europe and the Middle East (Chair)
Joint Economic Committee
**Joint Committee on the Organization of
Congress (Co-Chair)**

104th Congress, 1995–96
**International Relations (Ranking
Minority Member)**
Joint Economic Committee
**Commission on Protecting and Reducing
Government Secrecy**

105th Congress, 1997–98
**International Relations (Ranking
Minority Member)**
Joint Economic Committee

With American Legion members, 1966

"It is very clear that our country's founders saw Congress as the foremost, dominant branch of our national government. They gave it most of the powers and had an impressive vision for what they clearly perceived as government's 'First Branch.'"

—Lee Hamilton

With the Dalai Lama, 1993

"As hard as it is to get to Congress, doing a good job once you're there is even harder. The key is respecting the system and figuring out how to make it work. Frequently you will find people in Congress with high ideals, good ideas, and considerable energy who nonetheless lose because they never figured out how to work the system to get things done. It takes being a good politician in the best sense of the word: that in the face of the diverse beliefs and opinions represented in Washington, you can work with your colleagues to build support for an idea and move it forward."

—LEE HAMILTON

Fredericksburg, Indiana, parade, 1990

"Lawmaking . . . simply means trying to understand the hopes, needs, dreams, and desires of the American people and translating that into public policy through the legislative process."

—Lee Hamilton

"The American political system is built to move slowly so that Congress can guard against hasty action, take the time it needs to gain public acceptance for courageous legislation, and balance carefully the disparate forces in the country. Working within such a system is not easy. It takes enormous political skill to forge majorities, make the necessary trade-offs, assuage egos, and accommodate the different points of view."

—LEE HAMILTON

Meeting with Fairmont Elementary schoolchildren about anti-drug program, 1989

"Our founders believed that the accumulation of power in any person or institution was dangerous and that balancing them off, one against the other, protected against tyranny. The challenge was to create a government that was powerful enough to act, but not with uncontrolled or unchecked power."

—LEE HAMILTON

Capitol, 1981

Local television interview in front of Jefferson, Indiana Marriott during district visit, 1970

"In the end, Congress is where the American people express themselves in all their diversity and come to some agreement on what to do about the problems of the day. If it doesn't work, then our republic doesn't work either."

—LEE HAMILTON

Speaking from podium at Iran-Contra hearings, 1987

"We have had many presidents but no kings, and the Congress is principally responsible for that. For more than two centuries Congress has preserved free government and prevented tyranny . . . but it fundamentally rests upon informed citizens who understand the essential nature of our system and participate in our civic life. That is how Congress truly works."

—LEE HAMILTON

Printed and bound by CPI Group (UK) Ltd, Croydon, CR0 4YY

14/04/2025

14656888-0001